A LOWCOUNTRY *Lady's Guide* *to* CRABBING

Published by Advantage, Charleston, South Carolina.
Member of Advantage Media Group.

ADVANTAGE is a registered trademark and the Advantage colophon is a trademark of Advantage Media Group, Inc.

Printed in the United States of America.

ISBN: 978-1-59932-075-5
LCCN: 2008926316

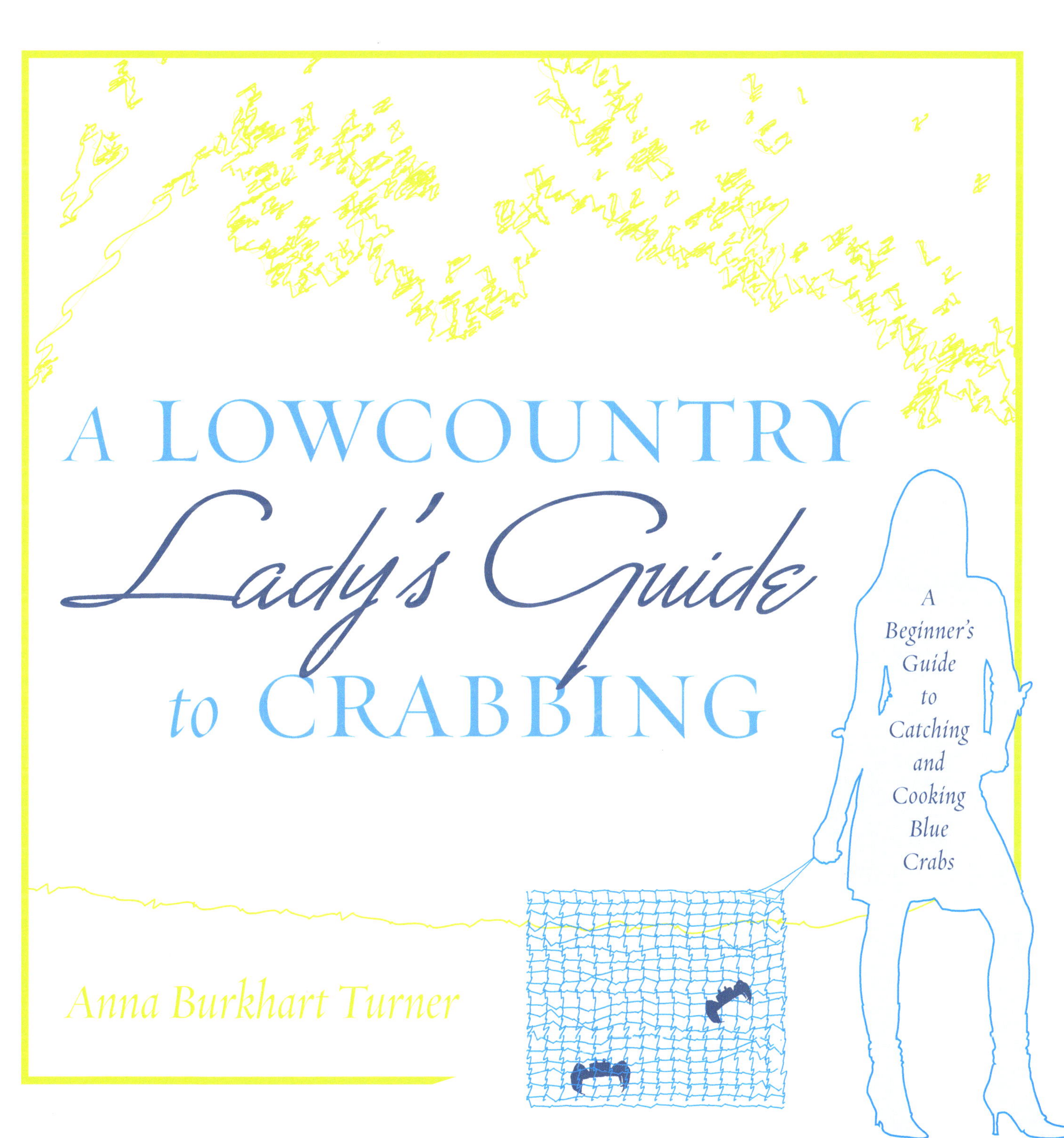

A LOWCOUNTRY *Lady's Guide* to CRABBING

A Beginner's Guide to Catching and Cooking Blue Crabs

Anna Burkhart Turner

Prologue

As spring approached, there was an increased desire to take up some type of hobby or outside activity. Sports were out, as I'm not the most athletic woman and who wants to get all hot and sweaty when it's boiling outside? I headed to the bookstore and decided I'd see what books I could find about fishing and crabbing.

There were plenty of books on fishing and a few on crabbing, and every single one assumed that either I knew something about fishing, bait, and tides, or had a big burley man on the cover. None of these would work. I didn't have any of the basic skills for these books, and it was concerning that every book assumed I was a man. So, women can't learn to go fishing and crabbing?

I am certainly not the only woman interested in learning these things. Ever since I've moved to Charleston, I've been intrigued by the true Lowcountry women who go fishing as soon as they get off work, the women who crab right off the side of their boat in the marsh, and the women who catch shrimp right off their dock. And these women are not exactly tomboys. How did these women learn to do this? After some more research, it seems to be a family tradition passed down through generations. The nature of the Coastal Carolinas is a huge part of life here, so it only makes sense that these ladies have mastered the skills of the great outdoors after years of adventures with their parents, siblings, and children.

This book is for those women who have never learned the art of crabbing or have not tried in years. It's a basic how-to-guide and assumes you know nothing about any kind of fishing, crabbing, or other southern sport. With this book, you will learn the crabbing traditions from the Santee to Hilton Head Island, so that you can pass it on to your friends and family. For those of you that do know how to crab, it will give you some new recipes from other Lowcountry ladies and some new tips on preparing and picking crab.

Everything in this book comes from my Lowcountry lady friends, who have taught me how to catch, clean, and cook blue crab. A special thanks to Janis and Ann Breazeale, the two true Lowcountry ladies that inspired this book. Thank you for teaching me about crabbing and sharing your stories with me. Thank you to my parents for continued encouragement, my husband Matt for keeping me laughing, and Pendleton for being my partner in crime on the crabbing adventures. Thank you to Kimberly, Deb, Jen, Stefanie, Patty, Mom, and Ann for allowing me to share your recipes. Thank you to Pendleton Shiflett for providing the illustrations for this book. And, of course, thanks to everyone Advantage Media for the continued encouragement and guidance.

Contents

Introduction

Slowing Down

We're running—sprinting actually—giving it our all to keep up with work, volunteer responsibilities, social engagements, and maintaining our health. It is so easy to forget to take a little "me time" every now and again. Time we need to reconnect and slow down. Time we need to remember the bigger picture. Learning new skills energizes us. It helps us to do our everyday tasks and shakes things up a bit. It makes us feel alive. So, you've already made it to step one. You've purchased this book to learn a new recipe, try your hand at crabbing, find a new activity for you and your family, or reconnect with the outdoors. Part of the reason I wrote this book was to learn a new skill myself. When I started, I had not been crabbing since I was a child. It's one of those things I found so much pleasure in, but stopped. I remember dropping the traps in the creek by my parent's beach house, filled with anticipation to see what we'd catch. The same excitement was there when I tried this same activity some twenty years later. With a girlfriend, we dropped the trap, enjoyed the view, and caught up on each other's lives. And, best of all, we caught giant crabs. We were excited and terrified all at the same time. The crabs, tangled in the netting of the trap, were really putting up a fight. With the tongs and some twisting and turning, we got the crabs into the cooler. We were living in the moment. So, whether you're interested in learning a new recipe, reliving your childhood, or being the protagonist in one of the famous Lowcountry novels by Dorthea Frank or Mary Alice Monroe, I hope you will find the thrill and fun in crabbing, learn the basics, and share the excitement with your friends. Enjoy!

Why Crabbing?

You're obviously intrigued to learn more about this cherished tradition of the Lowcountry and, of course, we all love to eat crab. The sweet meat found in a variety of dishes can send your head spinning in a state of euphoria. There are more recipes than you can imagine that include crab. Catching crabs will provide meat for fresh crab cakes, she crab soup, and countless other delectable dishes.

One of the most enjoyable aspects of crabbing is being outdoors and experiencing the true beauty of South Carolina's salt marshes and coastline. The marshes, bays, rivers, creeks, and ocean are beautiful pieces of nature we often overlook. Crabbing requires a good amount of patience and gives you time to enjoy the beauty of the Lowcountry with your friends and family. The smell of sweet pluff mud

and tidal creek water overloads the senses, and we are reminded there is more to this world than our schedules and our every day to-do lists. Time slows and you are allowed the rare opportunity to simply enjoy the place we South Carolinians call home.

Crabbing is a wonderful tool to learn about the unique ecosystem here in the Lowcountry. Along the pluff mud shoreline, you will see great blue herons, hermit crabs, snails, turtles, and, of course, blue crabs. The coastal plains and the salt marsh have unique habitats and animals due to the constant changing tides. Plants and animals have both adapted to survive in this ever-changing environment. If your interested is piqued after a couple crabbing trips, head to the South Carolina Aquarium to learn more about these regions and the resident plants and animals of South Carolina.

The Basics of Crabbing

The Blue Crab

The blue crab's scientific name is *callinectes sapidus*, meaning beautiful swimmer. They have two large claws on the front of their bodies. The remaining back legs are used to assist the crab in swimming and walking. The two fifth legs on each side have a flat, paddle-like shape to aid in swimming and mobility. Blue crabs live in the South Carolina coast's salt marshes, rivers, creeks, and ocean. Blue crabs become less active after the water drops below fifty degrees Fahrenheit.

South Carolina History

Blue crabs have been cherished by Lowcountry residents throughout history. The blue crab dates back to the days when Indians inhabited the coast. Indians caught their food in the woods and creeks along the coast, and they enjoyed crab as we do today in a variety of dishes. In the mid-nineteenth century, it is said the first she-crab soup was served in Charleston. Today, crabbing is enjoyed by many as a recreational sport. Additionally, commercial crabbing supports the South Carolina economy today. Commercial crabbing focuses on hard-shell blue crabs, as well as soft-shell crabs and annually brings in several million dollars to our economy.

The Lowcountry

Lowcountry is a term used to describe the coastal and island region of South Carolina, specifically south of the fall line down to St. Helena Island. The Lowcountry ranges from Hilton Head and Port Royal, through Edisto Island and the Charleston area, to Pawley's Island and Georgetown area. There is some discussion on where the Lowcountry ends. For the purpose of this book, we've included the Myrtle Beach and Grand Strand area when talking about the Lowcountry.

Male v. Female

You can tell the difference between a male and female crab by looking at the apron (underside of crab's shell). Males (Figure 1) will have a pencil shape design (skinny, vertical orientation) and females (Figure 2) will have the apron design (wide, triangular orientation). Females will have orange tips to their claws (Figure 3), while the males have blue tips (Figure 4). Essentially, the females have their "nails" painted orange. Mature females are called "sooks." Males are called "Jimmies." Immature females are called "she-crabs." She-crabs are typically smaller and have a less developed apron design, which is not as wide as the apron design of a sook.

Figure 1

Figure 2

Figure 3

Figure 4

Soft-shell Crab

As blue crabs grow, they shed their hard exoskeleton. Underneath the hard shell, the crab produces a new soft shell, which takes several days to harden completely. Soft shell crabs are a rarity to catch when crabbing. If you catch one, keep it! They make a great po-boy sandwich.

The Best Bait

Blue crabs are considered scavengers – meaning they'll eat just about anything that comes their way. Chicken is the most popular bait used for recreational crabbing. Many people use chicken necks, but the man at the Mt. Pleasant Piggy Wiggly informed me chicken backs work just as well.

As foul as it may be, the rule of thumb is: the stringier and fattier the bait, the better. Drumsticks and breast meat can be substituted as well.

Let's Go Crabbing – Materials

- **Crab tongs ($5) – or can be substituted with kitchen/salad tongs**
- **Double ring trap ($5-$10)**
- **Hand line with metal hook for bait/chicken ($3-$5)**
- **Crab pot ($25-$45 depending on style)**
- **6 necks or backs ($2)**
- **Long handle net ($10)**
- **Small weight to attach to double ring trap ($1-2)**
- **Cooler**
- **Ziploc bags**
- **Ice**
- **Scissors**
- **String**

Shop 'Til You Drop

Tackle and bait shops will have all the materials you'll need for crabbing. Many grocery stores and retail chains near the water and even hardware stores will carry the materials you'll need. Usually, there is small portion of an aisle dedicated to crabbing. Don't be intimidated to ask someone for help. Some of the best resources for me were the employees of these stores. Not only do they know how, they often know the "hot spots" for crabbing in your area with accessible parking.

Tick Tock

Although it's often argued among crabbers, it's believed the best time to crab are within two hours of high tide. That is not to say that you won't be able to catch crabs during the low tide. But, this is a great rule of thumb if you are unfamiliar with an area or unsure of how low tides get at your spot. Some creeks may be completely dry during low tide; crabbing within two hours of high tide will ensure you have some water. Remember: blue crabs are less active when the water drops below fifty degrees Fahrenheit, so make sure the waters are warm before you plan a crabbing trip.

Where to Crab?

The best places are on the salt marsh, inlets, or around jetties at the beach. Crabs have natural protection and food in these areas, making it their preferred place to reside. Crab off jetties, marsh docks, or under bridges running over the marsh. Again, be sure to check the tide charts if you are planning to crab in the creeks of the salt marshes. Many of the creeks are non-existent at low tide. You don't want to leave a pot full of yummy crabs basking in the sun on a mud-flat, now do you?

The Salt Marsh

According to the South Carolina Aquarium, twenty-five percent of the salt marshes on the east coast are in South Carolina. The salt marsh is an amazing place. The plants and animals must be able to live in brackish water. Water is combining from the incoming tides (salt water) with water flowing from the rivers (fresh water). Also, animals and plants must be able to live and co-exist within an environment of constant change. Every twelve hours, the tide changes from low to high.

The Usual Suspects

Inhabitants of the salt marsh:

- **Diamondback Terrapin**
- **Salt Marsh Snails**
- **Periwinkles**
- **Great Blue Heron**
- **Little Blue Heron**
- **Night Heron**
- **Fiddler Crabs**
- **Oysters**
- **Fish (Sheepshead, Pinfish, etc.)**

Things to Know Before Getting Started

South Carolina Crabbing Regulations

In South Carolina, the crabbing regulations are managed by the Department of Natural Resources. Visit their website for more information **www.dnr.sc.gov.**

Size Matters – In South Carolina, blue crabs must be at least five inches long, tip to tip of the shell. Smaller crabs should be thrown back so that they can grow larger.

Identify Yourself – In South Carolina, your crab pot must display your name. Your pot will be underwater, so a metal tag of identification on your rope is a good idea. Crabbing with more than two pots at a time will require a commercial crabber's license. Contact the Department of Natural Resources for more information.

Baby-on-Board – Crabs carrying eggs are not for "catch." You can identify a crab carrying eggs by looking at the apron of the female crab (underside of shell). A chain of orange eggs (called a "sponge") across the apron means she needs to be thrown back unharmed. This is to conserve the blue crab population.

Transporting and Storing Live Crabs

You should consider how in the world you are going to get your delicious live crabs back to your kitchen. It is very important they are alive when you cook them! Bacteria spreads quickly in crabs, so transporting live crabs correctly is essential. The best way to transport crabs is to fill several large Ziploc bags with ice. Seal and place the bags in the bottom of the cooler. This is important, because as the ice melts the crabs will not use up all of the oxygen in the water and die. The water will be contained in the baggie. Ice will also trigger the crabs to go into a sleep-like state. This will also make the crabs easier to deal with back in the kitchen.

Crabbing Methods

String and Neck (aka Hand Line)

A popular way of crabbing is with a string and chicken neck. A slab of chicken necks (unfortunately, it's as gross as it sounds) can be picked up at any grocery store. Use a regular string or a specially designed string with a hook for the meat ($3-$5 available at most tackles stores). First, select and appropriate location. String and neck is great for the beach, creeks running into the surf, bays or sounds. The water needs to be easily accessible and semi-calm. Secure the chicken neck to the string. You may need to tie several knots around the chicken to secure it. Step into the water. Throw the line with the chicken neck securely attached as far as possible. Let the line sit for a five to ten minutes. Then, slowly pull the string closer to shore over several minutes. Look for the weight of the chicken to feel heavier. The hope is that the crab is hanging onto the meat, not knowing it is being pulled closer to shore. If you see a crab feasting on the chicken, bring a longneck net in to swoop up the crab (from behind if possible). This is called "dipping." Place the crab in the cooler. The chicken will get soggy quickly, so it's a good idea to replace the piece with a new neck every ten to fifteen casts if you are not having luck or when it begins to deteriorate.

Crab Pots

Pots are by far the best method for crabbing when you are limited on time or aren't interested in checking the net or trap every couple of minutes. This is a no fuss, no mess

method. You can drop your pot and leave for a period of time. The pot does need to be checked every hour or so. Laws vary, so check how many pots you can have at a time. In the state of South Carolina, you can have up to two pots at a time and each pot must display your name. Believe me, you will catch plenty of crabs with just one pot, so two is really enough for casual crabbing.

How does it work?

Using a crab pot is probably one of the best ways to crab with less time and better results. Pots can be purchased anywhere you find fishing supplies. A crab pot is usually a large cube made out of chicken wire or wire netting covered with plastic with two to four entrances for crabs. There is also a center "chicken chamber" hanging from the top or bottom of the pot into the middle of the pot to attract crabs. Crabs will swim into the pot trying to get to the bait in the chamber. The entrances start out wide and get smaller and smaller as you move toward the center of the pot. The crab squeezes through and drops into the pot and feasts on the bait. The crab cannot get out, as the tapered entrances are too small and at an angle going back the other way. It sounds confusing, but just know the crabs are in your pot to stay.

Leaving a crab pot unattended

Do not leave a crab pot, unless you have a turtle excluder device (TED) on your pot. Not only do you attract crabs, but recently many turtles have been found dead in pots. The diamondback terrapins were once endangered after being used in the infamous turtle soup recipes decades ago. These beautiful creatures are indigenous to the salt marshes in the Lowcountry. Although they can stay underwater, terrapin turtles have lungs and need to air to breathe. To protect these animals, we must be responsible crabbers. For more information on turtle excluder devices for crab pots or diamondback terrapins, contact the South Carolina Aquarium at **www.sca.org** or DNR **www.dnr.sc.gov.**

Who are the diamondback terrapins?

Diamondback terrapins live in our salt marshes in South Carolina. They are light brown to black in color and have rings of color on their shell. Their head and feet are yellowish-green to white. Diamondback terrapins play a vital role in the salt marsh ecyosystem. They eat snails, fish, plants, worms, and crabs. They were a delicacy used in soup in the early twentieth century. After almost being wiped out, they've made a comeback. And now, they are facing another challenge. We need to do our best job to respect nature.

What is a TED?

The TEDs for crab pots are plastic rectangles for crabbers to fasten to the openings of their crab pots. The TEDs make it difficult for the turtles to get into the pot due to the way they rotate their bodies while swimming. Even with the TEDs, studies have show that crabs have no problem getting in and the use of TEDs does not decrease the number of crabs caught. The TEDs can be reused over and over with your pot.

How do I get a TED?

Many retailers in the Lowcountry have TEDs available. Make sure to ask when purchasing your crab pot.

Materials:

- **Crab pot ($15-$40 depending on style)**
- **Crab tongs**
- **Bait (3-4 packs of chicken necks or other to fill chamber)**
- **Thick, long rope (This rope will be significantly thicker than the very thin rope that you use with "string and neck method" and even the double ring trap method. This is to ensure you tie the pot to the dock and the string is sturdy enough to maintain the pot and not let it float away with a strong current.)**

Getting started

The best locations for crabbing with a pot are docks and bridges over waterways and creeks. Open the chamber in the middle of the pot. Fill the chamber with bait. Close the chamber. Attach a string to the top of the pot. Make sure this is attached well and tight. Make sure your name is attached somewhere to your pot or string. Drop your pot into the water, and tie off the rope to a secure location. Check your pot within the hour. If there are crabs in the pot, use the tongs to remove the crabs. Remember, toss back the undersized crabs (under five inches tip of the shell to tip of the shell) so that they can grow and mature to full size. Keep the full size crabs. Place the good crabs in the cooler.

Double Ring Net

Crabbing with a double ring net is one of the easiest methods and is a preferred method for children. It is great for children, because it is extremely easy to prepare and often a successful way for children to crab. Only certain locations will work well with a double ring net. The most successful locations will be docks and bridges over creeks, marsh or waterways. After dropping the net off the dock, the double ring net lays flat on the bottom of the creek floor. The crab will move over the flat basket to eat the bait. When you pull up the net, it will return to a basket-like shape. The crab is unable to escape. Although this is an easy method, this is not the best method if you do not want to tend to your crab net. Whereas you can leave a crab pot for an extended period of time, you'll need to check your double ring net periodically to remove the crabs. Otherwise, you may have some crabs feasting on your bait and then leaving.

To start, secure a chicken to the inside bottom of the net with a piece of twine. If there is a strong current, attach a small fishing weight to the bottom of the net. This will ensure the net makes it to the creek floor. Find the hook at the top of the basket-like net. Tie the end of your line to the net securely. Drop the net off the dock, and secure the rest of the line to a beam on the dock or bridge. Wait five to ten minutes. Quickly pull the net up out of the water. If a crab is in the net, use the crab tongs to remove it and place it in the cooler on ice. The crab will try to defend itself, so crab tongs are suggested to decrease the likelihood of getting pinched. Crab tongs will give you a safe distance to pick up the crab and get it into the cooler.

Using a double ring method is a game of chance. The best part about it is guessing if there is a crab in your net. Some people say you can feel if a crab is nibbling on the chicken. However, the current can cause this as well. The only real way to know is to yank up the net and check.

Conservation

It is important for us all to think about taking care of our environment and the true wonders of the Lowcountry. There are many simple things we can do, and educate others to do. Below are some great tips on how we can contribute and preserve our natural resources.

Top Ten Easy Ways to Make a Difference:

1. Take only what you need for your recipe or your plans.
2. Never leave crab pots unattended, unless you use a turtle excluder device. This is to ensure terrapins don't end up trapped in the pot.
3. Always pick up your trash! Often, the beautiful sea turtles that nest on the beaches in South Carolina try to eat trash, thinking it is a jellyfish or some other type of food.
4. Turn of your lights if you live on the beach during the summer. When baby sea turtles hatch, they head to the water using the moon as a guide. Often bright lights at the beach can confuse them and get them going in the wrong direction.
5. Always follow the regulations! For crabbing in South Carolina, this means throwing back crabs smaller than five inches or crabs carrying eggs.
6. Teach others! The best thing you can do to help the conservation of the Lowcountry is to teach others about conservation and respect for the environment.
7. Retrieve tangled lines, broken crab pots, etc. Leaving this in the salt marsh or on the beach is another form of litter. It can also be hazardous to the animals.
8. Give your time, money, and support to local organizations whose missions support conservation and educate the public on conservation.
9. When beachcombing, always look inside shells before you take them home. You never know who is living inside. Throw back any shells with active residents.
10. Stay off the dunes. They provide a natural barrier against wind and water erosion. And, it's the law!

Low Country Crabbing Attire

Of course, it always feels great to look fabulous! In addition to looking good for the sake of looking good, you'll need certain attire to make your crabbing adventure a success. So, let's discuss the do's and don'ts of crabbing fashion. Flip flops are key, as you'll be in and out of the water frequently. Your ensemble should allow for you to get in the water easily. Skirts and dresses may be cute, but you'll have a difficult time climbing on the jetties to retrieve a snagged line or catch that crab. Skorts (yes, skorts) or tennis skirts provide comfort and fashion for crabbing. They look adorable, while providing the flexibility to move freely. Capris or shorts also work well. Also, make sure you have pockets in your shorts or you wear an anorak with pockets. You'll be carrying scissors, crabbing line, and anti-bacterial gel with you. It can be a real pain to have to go back to your beach bag several times to get stuff once you've ventured into the water. Some type of hat and sunscreen are essential. The sun is very powerful on the water in the Lowcountry. If you don't already know that, you soon will. Wear sunscreen even when it is cloudy. The shade of a sun hat, sunscreen and sunglasses all prevent signs of aging and skin cancers. According to dermatologists and the cancer prevention groups, you should be wearing at least 30 SPF with zinc oxide or Parasol 1789 as an active ingredient. If you will be wading out into the salt marsh, slip on a pair of old tennis shoes, aqua socks or wading boots. Oyster beds in the salt marshes are often underneath the pluff mud and the sharp edges of the shells can really injure someone.

Crabbing is Sexy?

Can you make crabbing sexy? Maybe not sexy outright, but it could make for a romantic date or outing. Yes, crabbing is romantic. Think about it… packing a mouthwatering picnic dinner and wine, checking your crabbing pot, eating on a blanket at the end of a secluded dock. As the sun sets and the sky turns to black, you watch the stars appear and hear the nocturnal sounds of nature as the salt marsh comes alive with frogs, turtles, insects, and owls. It's a running joke that the South Carolina's state bird is the mosquito. So, if you venture out, plan on bringing the citronella candles and bug spray. And, if you plan a crabbing date, make sure it is at high tide. Pluff mud is exposed during low tide in the salt marsh. It is made up of decomposing matter, and can have a less than appetizing smell.

Making a Crab Boil

A popular event on the East Coast is a crab boil. This is a great way to get your friends together and share one of your great catches. Typically, crab boils are very informal. Newspaper is spread across a table. In a large pot, the cook boils blue crabs, corn, and sausage. After draining the cooked mixture, the contents of the pot are dumped onto the table. The participants eat all the delicious food with their hands – no utensils allowed, though the guests are given wooden hammers to crack open the crabs. Crab boils are a great event for late summer evenings for people of all ages. See the recipes section for more details.

Crabbing Resources

Crabbing Gear and Equipment

ne of the best resources for learning about crabbing is your local bait and tackle shop. The people working in these shops are passionate about the outdoors, and they will be able to help you find the items you need for a successful crabbing trip. While you are there, consider asking them for directions to some of the local crabbing spots.

We've included a list of some of our favorite supply shops:

- **Seewee Outpost**
  4853 Highway 17 North
  Awendaw, SC 29429
  (843) 928-3493

- **Bull's Bay Supply**
  10086 North Highway 17
  McClellanville, SC 29458
  (843) 887-3251

- **Beaufort Marine Supply Incorporated**
  105 Savannah Highway
  Beaufort, SC 29906
  (843) 525-1611

- **Hadrell's Point Bait and Tackle**
  885 Ben Sawyer Boulevard
  Mt. Pleasant, SC 29464
  (843) 881-3644

- **Folly Beach Pier**
  101 East Arctic Avenue
  Folly Beach, SC 29439
  (843) 588-3474

- **The Pier at Garden City**
  110 South Waccamaw Drive
  Garden City Beach, SC 29576
  (843) 651-9700

- **Surfside Pier**
  11 South Ocean Boulevard
  Surfside Beach, South Carolina 29575
  (843) 238-0121

- **The Charleston Angler**
  654 Saint Andrews Boulevard
  Charleston, SC 29407
  (843) 571-3899

- **Pawley's Island Supplies**
  10460 Ocean Highway
  Pawley's Island, SC
  (843) 237-2912

- **The Red and White Grocery Store**
  1513 Palm Boulevard
  Isle of Palms, SC 29451
  (843) 886-6250

Public Parks for Crabbing

- **Daniel Island – Charleston**
- **Edisto Beach State Park – Edisto**
- **Hampton Plantation State Historic Site – McClellanville**
- **Hunting Island State Park – Beaufort**
- **Huntington Beach State Park – Murrells Inlet**
- **Breach Inlet – Isle of Palms**
- **Myrtle Beach State Park – Myrtle Beach**
- **North Inlet, Winyah Bay – Georgetown**

Educational Learning Centers in the Lowcountry

South Carolina Aquarium – Charleston, SC

Coastal Discovery Museum – Hilton Head, SC

The Lowcountry Estuarium – Port Royal, SC

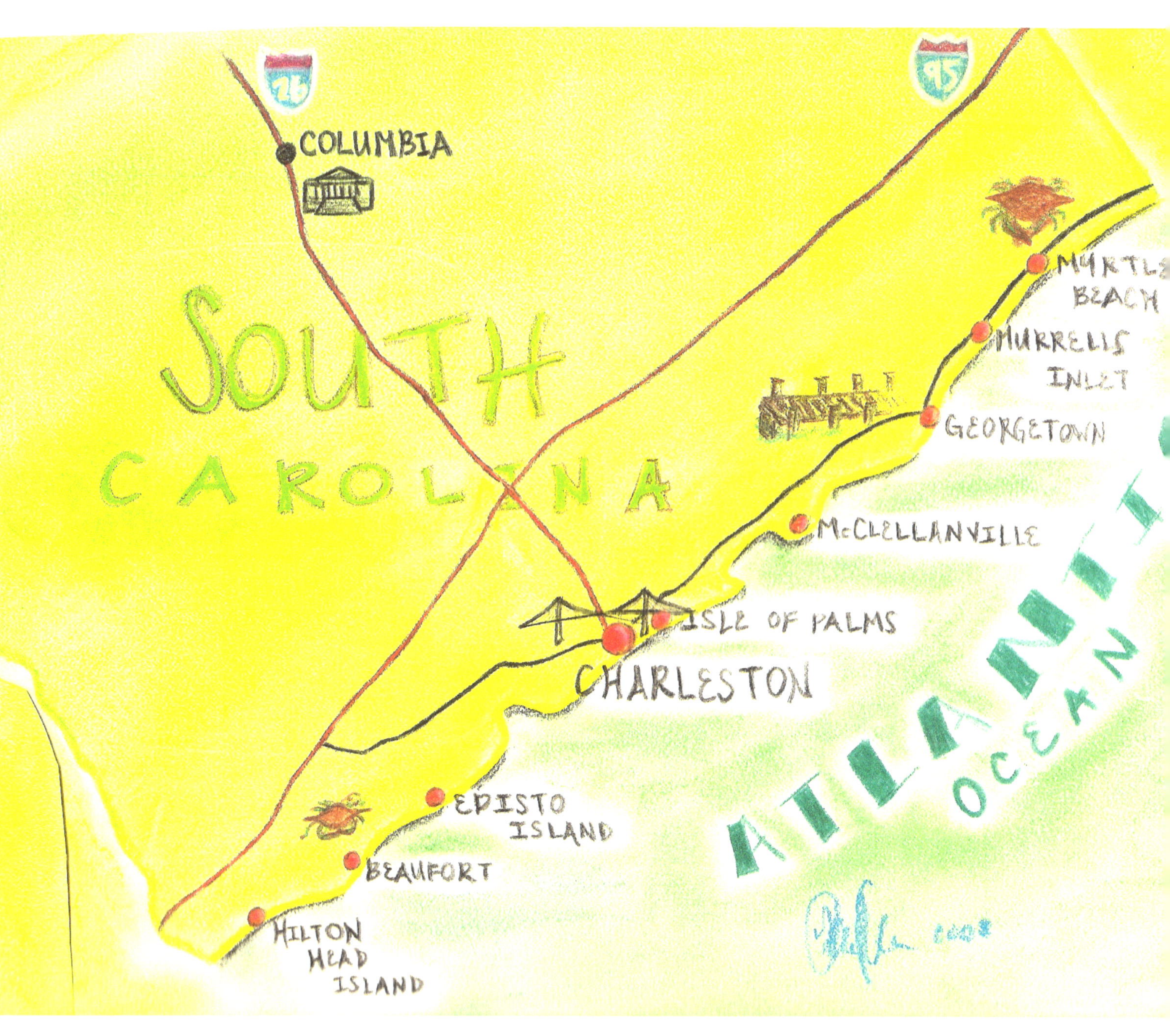

26
95
COLUMBIA
SOUTH
CAROLINA
MYRTL
BEACH
MURRELLS
INLET
GEORGETOWN
McCLELLANVILLE
ISLE OF PALMS
CHARLESTON
EDISTO
ISLAND
BEAUFORT
HILTON
HEAD
ISLAND
OCEAN

Crabbing Glossary

Like anything, crabbing has its own terminology. Use this quick guide to help you get acclimated to this activity and to impress your friends.

- **Apron** – the underside of a crab
- **Callinectes Sapidus** – the scientific name for the blue crab meaning beautiful swimmer
- **Crab Pot** – metal cube or pyramid used to catch crabs, typically dropped from piers or docks
- **Crab Trap** – net made of two double rings used to catch crabs, typically dropped from piers or docks
- **Diamondback Terrapin** – an endangered species of turtle indigenous to the Lowcountry
- **Dipping** – using a long handled net to catching crabs visible in the water
- **Hand Line** – a style of crabbing using a piece of string with a metal hook at the end for bait. The line is pulled slowly through the water to attract crabs
- **Jimmy** – a male crab
- **Lowcountry** – term used to describe the coastal region of South Carolina spanning from the southern coastal islands of Hilton Head to Pawley's Island and Georgetown area
- **Salt Marsh** – home to the blue crabs
- **She-crab** – an immature female crab
- **Soft-shell Crab** – a blue crab which has recently molted, leaving a soft-shell taking several days to harden
- **Sook** – a mature female crab
- **Sponge** – term to describe the orange eggs of a female crab draped across the apron
- **TED (Turtle Excluder Device)** – a plastic rectangle place on the openings of crab pots to deter turtles from being caught

Annual Lowcountry Outdoor Events

South Carolinians love their crabs. Crabbing festivals and other related events happen annually and are great fun for all ages. You'll see everything from cooking demonstrations to arts and crafts. If you'll be in the lowcountry during these times, make every effort to attend one of these local events. For a current listing of crabbing festivals, visit **www.learn-to-crab.com/festivals**

- **January**
  Boone Hall Oyster Festival – Mount Pleasant
- **February**
  Southeastern Wildlife Expedition – Charleston
- **April**
  Soft Shell Crab Festival – Port Royal
  Blessing of the Fleet – Mount Pleasant
- **May**
  Little River Blue Crab Festival – Little River
  Lowcountry Shrimp Festival and Blessing of the Fleet – McClellanville
- **August**
  Annual Blue Crab Festival – Awendaw, SC
- **September**
  Charleston Shrimpin' and Shagging Festival – Charleston, SC

Additional Resources

Consider checking out the following resources for more information on topics not covered in detail in this book:

- **The South Carolina Aquarium**
  www.sca.org
- **The Department of Natural Resources**
  www.dnr.sc.gov
- **Tide Charts**
  www.sciway.net/weather/tides
- **Learn-to-Crab**
  www.learn-to-crab.com
- **State Parks of SC**
  www.southcarolinaparks.com/maps
- **The Blue Crab**
  www.dnr.sc.gov/marine/pub/seascience/bluecrab

Preparin' and Pickin' the Crabs

Nothing is more succulent than fresh crabmeat in an omelet, crab cakes, or in making she-crab soup. So, now that you've got a ton of crabs, you're ready to try cooking them.

First, you've got to cook up those crabs you've kept alive. This is the preferred method, as we mentioned, bacteria in dead crabs spreads fast. Some pros clean the crabs while alive, but for us beginners, it best to stick with cooked crabs. There is a high risk of getting pinched while cleaning live crabs—as you can imagine.

Cooking Crabs

Bacteria spread quickly in dead crabs. Although crabs on ice go into a hibernation-like state, they will move frantically before going in the pot of boiling water. If a crab does not move, throw it away. Do not cook a dead crab.

- **Bring 2 gallons of water to a boil.**
- **Add one full beer.**
- **Add 2 tablespoons of Old Bay Seasoning.**
- **Place live crabs one by one in the boiling water. The best way to do this is to transport each crab from the cooler into the boiling water with crab tongs. Although the crabs seem dormant while in the cooler, they will get rowdy.**
- **Cover the pot and cook for 25 minutes. Crabs will turn pink after being placed in the water and appear rusty orange or red after being cooked.**

Cleaning the Crabs

Before creating your masterpiece meals, you've got some cleaning to do. And, this is a great group activity. With a group of friends or family turn on some tunes, and sit around the table to begin cleaning! It takes a lot of effort to get a little meat, but it is well worth it.

Charleston Crab Picker Method

Many years ago, there was a crab plant in Charleston. The pickers taught a couple of Charleston ladies how to pick crabs to get the most meat out of a crab. This method came straight from the crab pickers. This method has been passed down among Lowcountry ladies for years, and now to you. Ann Lockwood Breazeale contributed this method.

Materials

- **Newspaper**
- **Two large bowls (one for crab meat, one for shells/limbs)**
- **Hammer**
- **Cooked crabs**
- **Knife**

Step 1: Twist off (clockwise) the claws and the legs. In order to save the most meat, do not pull while you are twisting. Throw away the legs. Set aside the claws.

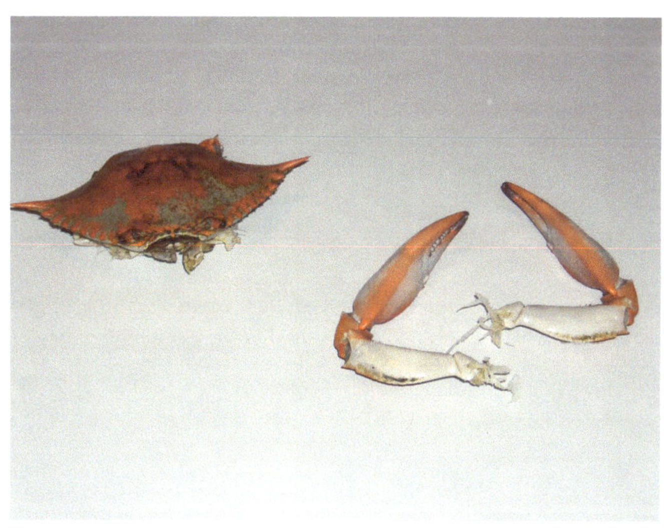

Step 2: Place your knife under the pencil or apron.

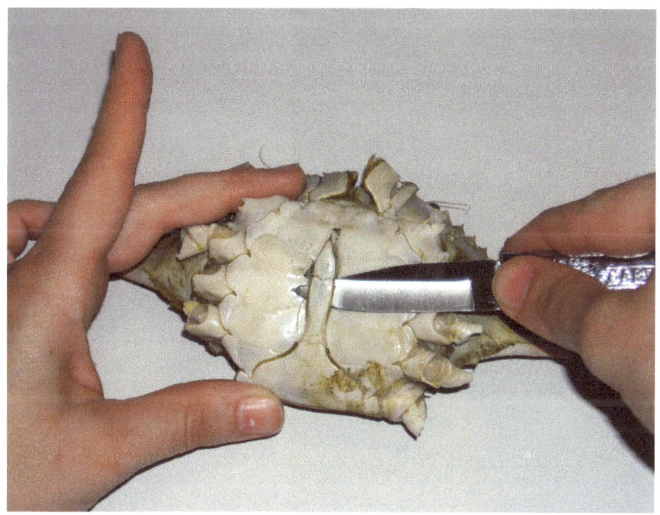

Pull back on this until the shell pops open

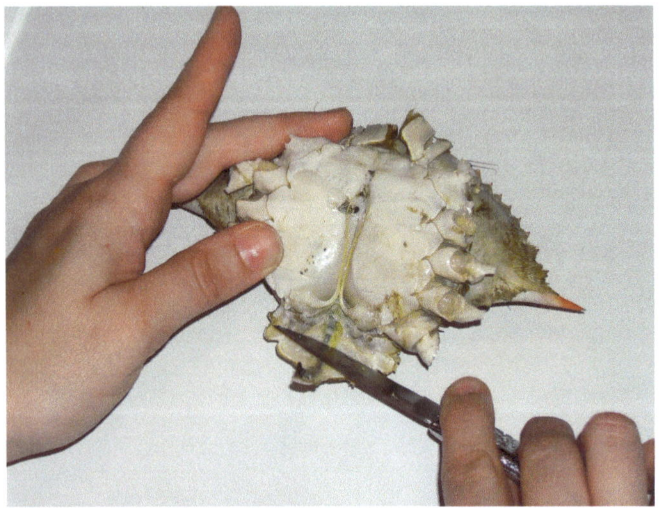

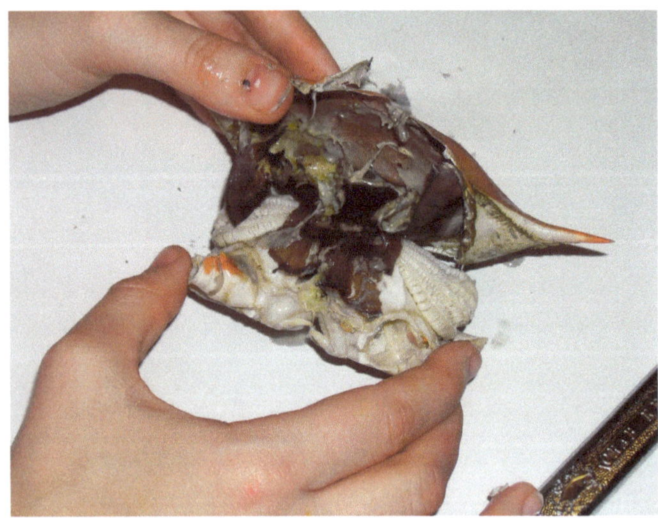

You should be left with two pieces – the outer top shell*, and the bottom core. The core will be significantly smaller and will fit in the palm of your hand.

Step 3: You will see some brown mush in the core. Rinse the brown mush away very carefully and thoroughly. This is like deveining a shrimp, but a bit messier.

Step 4: Place the knife vertically across the core

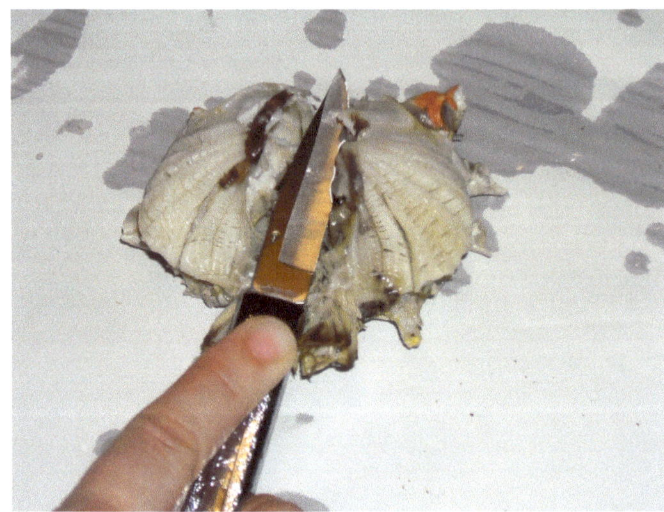

(leg openings should be on the left and right) with the blade to the side. The core should be "soft side" up. Pull the knife through the left leg openings evenly. Repeat on the right side.

Step 5: There are now three pieces. Use your fingers to clean out each chamber full of meat. Place the meat in your lump crabmeat bowl.

Step 6: Take a claw. Lightly hammer the claw. With your fingers, delicately break open the claw and remove the meat. Place meat in the claw crab bowl. Repeat with remaining claw.

Step 7: Sift through the meat with your hands to check for any crab shells. This can easily ruin a meal, so be thorough. Set aside crabmeat to use in a recipe.

*Saving the outer shell: some people save the outer shell to use as a bowl for individual deviled crabs or arts and crafts (i.e. Christmas tree ornaments). If you'd like to use the outer shell for something, rinse it out very well and set aside to dry.

How many crabs do you need for a pound of crabmeat?

Eighteen to twenty mid size crabs will make a pound of crabmeat.

Saving the Leftovers

Only freeze crabmeat once. If you buy frozen crab, you can't cook it and then refreeze it for later. Fresh crab can be frozen and will last sixty to ninety days in the freezer. The best thing to do is use fresh crabmeat to make your meal. Then, freeze several portions individually to thaw for another day.

What to Do With All that Meat?

Lowcountry Lady Recipes

The best crab recipes from around the area have been compiled in the remaining section. Everything from casseroles to dips is here, as well as information about the contributor. Enjoy trying different recipes with your fresh catch or purchase store bought crabmeat for the following recipes.

Crabby Mac N' Cheese

From the Kitchen of: Stefanie Greene

Great for both kids and adults!

Ingredients:

- **1 lb. elbow, penne, or shell macaroni**
- **8 oz. shredded cheddar cheese (add some gouda or parmesan cheese to create a richer sauce)**
- **4 oz. crabmeat or imitation crab (lobster may also be added to the dish)**
- **3 tbsp. butter**
- **dash of Old Bay seasoning**

Directions:

1. Cook pasta aldente. Spray casserole dish with cooking spray.
2. Place pasta in casserole dish.
3. Melt butter and pour over pasta. Set aside and cover to keep warm.
4. Finely chop crabmeat. Mix crab/lobster with pasta.
5. Top with cheddar cheese (and/or gouda/parmesan).
6. Heat in oven at 350 degrees for twenty minutes or until cheese is nicely melted.
7. Sprinkle with Old Bay seasoning and pepper.

Servings: 4

Crabmeat Delights

From the Kitchen of: Deb Herman

Ingredients:

- **½ cup butter, softened**
- **1 (5 oz.) jar Old English cheese spread**
- **1 ½ tsp. mayonnaise**
- **½ tsp. garlic salt**
- **7 oz. crabmeat, drained**
- **6 English muffins split in quarters**

Directions:

1. Mix butter and cheese with mayonnaise and garlic salt. Stir in crabmeat.
2. Spread on muffins. Freeze at least ten minutes.
3. Remove from freezer, cut into quarters and broil five to ten minutes until hot and bubbly. Serve warm.

May be made ahead and frozen until ready to broil.

Crabmeat Supreme Spread

From the Kitchen of: Deb Herman

Ingredients:

- **12 oz. cream cheese, softened**
- **juice of one lemon**
- **2 tbsp. mayonnaise**
- **1 tsp. Worcestershire sauce**
- **1 medium onion chopped very fine**
- **dash of garlic powder**
- **7 oz. lump crabmeat, drained**

Directions:

1. Mix above ingredients and place on attractive serving plate.
2. Cover ½ bottle cocktail sauce.
3. Add shredded crabmeat on top of cocktail sauce.
4. Cover and refrigerate for twenty-four hours. Serve with crackers.

Crab Quiche

From the Kitchen of: Kimberly Jackson

This is a great basic quiche recipe. You can substitute the crabmeat for a different quiche, such as sausage or spinach and use a variety of cheeses.

Ingredients:

- **1 deep-dish frozen pie shell**
- **½ cup mayonnaise**
- **2 tbsp. all-purpose flour**
- **2 eggs, beaten**
- **½ cup milk**
- **8 oz. lump crabmeat**
- **1 (8 oz.) package shredded Swiss cheese**
- **¼ cup chopped green onion**
- **dash of basil (fresh or dried), salt and pepper**

Directions:

1. Preheat oven to 350°F. Combine mayonnaise, flour, eggs and milk. Stir until well blended. Add the crabmeat, cheese, green onion, basil, salt and pepper.
2. Pour into pie shell and bake for forty to forty-five minutes.

Crab and Cheese Casserole

From the Kitchen of: Deb Herman

Ingredients:

- **1 lb. Old English cheese**
- **8 slices white bread (no crusts)**
- **5 eggs**
- **1 pint milk**
- **½ cup melted butter**
- **7 oz. crabmeat, drained**

Directions:

1. Break bread and cheese in pieces and mix.
2. Grease casserole dish well. Alternate bread and cheese with layer of crabmeat ending with bread and cheese on top.
3. Beat eggs; add milk and butter. Pour over mixture. You may add can of mushrooms, if desired.
4. Bake in pan in oven for one hour at 350. May be prepared the night before and refrigerated.

Petite Crab Cakes

From the Kitchen of: Patty Turner

Serve these with various dipping sauces; it's a great way to begin a party.

Ingredients:

- **1 lb. lump crabmeat**
- **1 egg, plus one yolk**
- **1/3 cup Duke's mayonnaise**
- **1 tbsp. spicy mustard**
- **¼ cup fresh parsley, finely diced**
- **1 tbsp. fresh dill**
- **¼ cup finely diced bell pepper**
- **1 tbsp. Old Bay seasoning**
- **1 tbsp. Worcestershire sauce**
- **Sea salt, freshly ground pepper and cayenne to taste.**
- **¼ cup fresh bread crumbs**
- **1 cup finely crushed herb crackers**
- **olive oil and butter**

Directions:

1. Preheat oven to 400° F.
2. Combine eggs, mayo, mustard, herbs, and all seasonings in a large bowl.
3. Stir in onion and bell pepper.
4. Add crab and breadcrumbs and combine.
5. Form cakes with small cookie scoop, coat in herb crackers, and chill for thirty minutes.
6. Heat oil and butter in sauté pan; brown cakes on both sides.
7. Place on baking sheet and bake for eight minutes.

Servings: 36 crab cakes

Crab Stuffed Mushrooms

From the Kitchen of: Deb Herman

Ingredients:

Marinade

- **2 cups oil**
- **¾ cup tarragon vinegar**
- **3 tbsp. sugar**

Stuffing

- **8 oz. cream cheese, softened**
- **½ cup sour cream**
- **½ cup mayonnaise**
- **½ cup onion grated**
- **½ bunch green onions chopped tops only**
- **2 garlic cloves, crushed**
- **2 tbsp. lemon juice**
- **½ lb. lump crabmeat**

Directions:

1. Remove stems from fifty large mushrooms.
2. Soak mushrooms overnight in marinade.
3. Combine ingredients for stuffing. Mix well.
4. Drain mushrooms. Fill each cap with stuffing and chill.

Baked Crab Dip

From the Kitchen of: Jen Volpe ~ Great for parties!

Ingredients:

- **1 (8 oz.) packages cream cheese, cut into 1-inch cubes**
- **¼ cup milk**
- **3 tbsp. fresh lemon juice**
- **2 tbsp. minced onion**
- **2 tsp. Worcestershire**
- **2 tsp. Dijon mustard**
- **1 ½ tsp. Old Bay seasoning**
- **1 tsp. Tabasco**
- **1 pound fresh or pasteurized crabmeat, squeezed dry and picked over**
- **2 tbsp. minced fresh parsley**

Directions:

1. Adjust the oven rack to the middle position and heat the oven to 475 degrees. Microwave the cream cheese in a large bowl on high power until very soft, twenty to thirty seconds. Whisk in the milk, lemon juice, onion, Worcestershire, mustard, Old Bay and Tabasco. Gently fold the crabmeat using a rubber spatula.
2. Transfer to a greased a one-quart baking dish. Bake until browned and bubbling – approximately twenty to twenty-five minutes. Cool for five minutes before sprinkling with parsley and serve.

Servings: 10

Serve with crackers

To Make Ahead:

The dip can be made through step one and refrigerated, wrapped tightly in plastic wrap, for up to twenty-four hours. Before continuing with step two, heat the dip in a microwave on high power until it begins to bubble around the edges, two to five minutes. Stir to combine, and then bake as directed in step two.

Vegetable and Crabmeat Casserole

From the Kitchen of: Nancy Burkhart

Serve with salad and rolls and, of course, iced tea with mint!

Ingredients:

- **1 can of Amy's Organic Soup**
- **1 cup of organic mushrooms (Shitake, or other)**
- **½ to 1 cup of unseasoned bread crumbs**
- **1 cup of lump crabmeat cooked**
- **1 lb. of a mixture of organic yellow and/or zucchini squash**
- **1 cup of corn (off the cob is best)**
- **2 tbsp. of lemon juice**
- **2 eggs or Eggbeaters (organic if possible)**
- **½ cup of grated organic mozzarella cheese (you can select another type, if you prefer)**

Directions:

1. Cut the vegetables of squash into one-inch pieces. Steam the squash, and corn for approximately four to five minutes.
2. Remove and add to the can of organic soup.
3. Add mushrooms, breadcrumbs, lemon juice and eggs.
4. Lastly, add the crab mixture. If mixture has too much liquid, you may want to add a few more breadcrumbs.
5. Toss mixture. Pour into a casserole dish and top with cheese.
6. Bake at 350 for twenty-five to thirty minutes. Tent with foil for the first twenty minutes but be sure that the foil is not touching the cheese.

Deviled Crab

From the Kitchen of: Ann Breazeale

A true southern tradition – this recipe has been passed down for generations.

Ingredients:

- **One pound lump crabmeat**
- **½ cup ketchup**
- **1 tube Ritz crackers**
- **½ bell pepper (chopped)**
- **2 eggs**

Directions:

1. Place crabmeat in bowl with Ritz crackers and bell pepper. Lightly toss by hand. Do not break crabmeat.
2. Add ketchup. Toss lightly by hand again. Mixture should begin to clump together.
3. Add eggs. Mixture should be the consistency of ground beef.
4. Make the mixture into patties. Place each patty on a cookie sheet, place a pat of butter on each, and bake at 325 for twenty to twenty-five minutes until golden brown.

Tip:

1. If patties are too moist, sprinkle extra Ritz on the bottom and top to keep patties together.
2. Re-fill crab shells (cleaned) with deviled crab for a fun twist on this recipe.

Servings: 4-6 crab patties

Crab Angels

From the Kitchen of: Anna Turner

Great appetizer for Thai or Chinese entrees

Ingredients:

- **1 (8 oz.) package of cream cheese**
- **1 tsp hot sauce**
- **1 scallion, finely chopped**
- **One lb. lump crabmeat**
- **1 package small, square wonton sheets (25-30)**
- **1 egg white**
- **1 tbsp. butter**

Directions:

1. Mix cream cheese, hot sauce and scallions together, and set aside.
2. Break up crabmeat with hands, and fold into cream cheese mixture.
3. Preheat oven to 350 degrees.
4. On a clean, dry surface, lay wonton sheets down. With a pastry brush, line the outer edge of the wonton lightly with egg.
5. Drop one teaspoon of the crab and cream cheese mixture into the center.
6. Fold the wonton diagonally to create a triangle. To seal the wontons, press a fork along the two open sides of the wonton. Next fold in the corners of each triangle.
7. Lightly grease a baking sheet with butter. Place completed wontons on the sheet.
8. Brush the wontons tops lightly with egg. Bake for eight minutes, or until lightly browned. Turn the wonton, and bake on the other side for an additional eight minutes.

Servings: 24 crab angels

Wontons are great as is, but you can add a side bowl of soy sauce or ginger dipping sauce for a twist. Instead of baking, wontons can also be fried in oil. Heat oil to 350 degrees in a deep fryer or heavy skillet. Cook each wonton for two to three minutes, turning once.

Crab and Shrimp Spring Rolls

From the Kitchen of: Anna Turner

Great appetizer for Thai or Chinese entree

Ingredients:

- **1 tbsp. toasted sesame oil**
- **1 cup finely shredded Napa cabbage**
- **1 cup grated carrot**
- **3 tbsp. green onions, chopped**
- **3 scallion, chopped**
- **1 tbsp. ginger, grated**
- **¼ cup breadcrumbs**
- **2 egg whites, divided**
- **3 tbsp. fresh basil, lightly chopped**
- **3 tbsp. cilantro, lightly chopped**
- **½ lb. pre-cooked shrimp, chopped**
- **1 lb. lump crabmeat**
- **1 package spring roll wrappers (24)**

Directions:

1. In a large pan, sauté the carrots and cabbage in the sesame oil for five minutes. Next, add the ginger, scallions, and green onions. Set aside to cool. Once cool, pour into a mixing bowl. Add breadcrumbs, one egg white, shrimp, basil, and cilantro. Fold in crabmeat.
2. Place the spring roll wrapper on a clean, dry surface. With a pastry brush, moisten the outer four edges of the spring roll with the egg white.
3. On the bottom of the spring roll wrapper, drop three tablespoons of mixture across the length of the spring roll. Leave a half-inch on each side free of filling.
4. Fold wrapper over the filling and tightly roll into a tube. Press the ends together to seal. Complete the same steps for all spring rolls.
5. In a skillet, fry spring rolls on each side for one and a half minutes. Serve with dipping sauce.

Servings: 24 spring rolls

Serve with a ginger soy dipping sauce. To make, combine a tablespoon of Tamari (natural soy sauce), a tablespoon of mirin (sweet rice wine), a teaspoon of grated ginger, and a quarter teaspoon of red curry paste.

Steamed crab with garlic dipping sauce

From the Kitchen of: Anna Turner

This delicious appetizer is as fun to eat as it is simple to prepare. It's definitely a "do it yourself" activity. It is great for those times when you may not be in the mood to pick the crabs yourself. This model can be used for a crab boil, as well.

Ingredients:

- **wooden hammer (4)**
- **strainer (fine)**
- **boiled crabs (12)**
- **2 sticks butter**
- **3 cloves garlic**
- **skillet**
- **small bowl**
- **2 tbsp. sugar**
- **knife**

Directions:

1. Roughly chop the garlic. Lightly brown garlic in a skillet with cooking spray on low setting.
2. Add two sticks of butter until melted.
3. Add two tablespoons of sugar and stir until dissolved.
4. Once dissolved, strain butter into a small dish. Serve with crabs and hammers.

Serving: 4

For an authentic crab boil, spread your newspaper over an outdoor table. Dump the steam crabs out, provide wooden hammers, and allow your guests to pick the crabs. Use a galvanized tub with ice to store beverages.

Soft shell Crab Po-Boy

From the Kitchen of: Anna Turner

A Po-Boy sandwich is an easy way to make a great meal out of a rare catch. Although it is rare to catch soft shell blue crabs, you can often purchase live soft-shell crabs from local seafood distributors.

Ingredients:

- **scissors**
- **2 cups whole milk**
- **3 eggs, beaten**
- **2 cups flour**
- **6 soft shell blue crabs**
- **6 Italian sub rolls**
- **1 head lettuce**
- **2 tomatoes**
- **mayonnaise**
- **2 bowls**
- **1 cup of oil (peanut or canola)**
- **tongs**
- **paper bag**
- **skillet**
- **lemon juice**

Preparation:

1. Keep the live soft shell crabs on ice until you area ready.
2. Cut off the face of the soft shell crab (about a half-inch in).
3. Next, remove the gills on both sides of the crab. The gills are on the left and right sides of the crab. Peel the gills back and cut off.
4. Lastly, remove the "tail" or "skirt" of the crab. To do this, trim the backside of the crab off.

Directions:

1. Heat the oil in a skillet. Oil should be about a half-inch to an inch high.
2. In one bowl, mix the eggs and the milk. In another bowl, place the flour.
3. Dip each crab into the milk/egg mixture. Coat both sides. Next, dip crab into the flour mixture. Coat both sides.
4. Place the crab in the hot oil. Cook until brown and crispy on each side.
5. Remove the cooked crab with tongs and place the crab on a paper bag. Sprinkle with fresh lemon juice.
6. Place the crab on the cut sub bread. Add lettuce, tomato, and mayonnaise.

Lowcountry Crab Boil

From the Kitchen of: Anna Turner

Gather your friends and have a party.

Ingredients:

- **large pot**
- **1 beer**
- **1 bag of new potatoes, halved**
- **2 packages of kielbasa sausage (cut into 1-inch pieces)**
- **8 ears of corn, halved**
- **6 blue crabs**
- **4 lbs. of shrimp**
- **Old Bay seasoning**
- **newspaper**
- **wooden hammers**

Directions:

1. Bring water to a rolling boil. Add beer. Add seasoning liberally.
2. Add potatoes and sausage. Cook for ten minutes.
3. Add corn and crab. Cook for five minutes.
4. Check to see if potatoes are done. They should be soft when punctured with a fork. Once potatoes are done, add the shrimp. Cook for two to three minutes.
5. Drain water out of the pot.
6. Dump the mixture on a table lined with newspapers. Provide wooden hammers for the crabs. Enjoy!

About the Author:

Anna Turner is the author of **www.learn-to-crab.com**, a beginner's online guide to catching and cooking blue crabs. She lives in Mount Pleasant, South Carolina and enjoys traveling, spending time outdoors and cooking. She additionally served for several years on the education team of a lowcountry aquarium as an exhibit guide.

www.ingramcontent.com/pod-product-compliance
Lightning Source LLC
LaVergne TN
LVHW070150110826
845147LV00002B/362